The War of Unsaid Things

By: Tori Wils

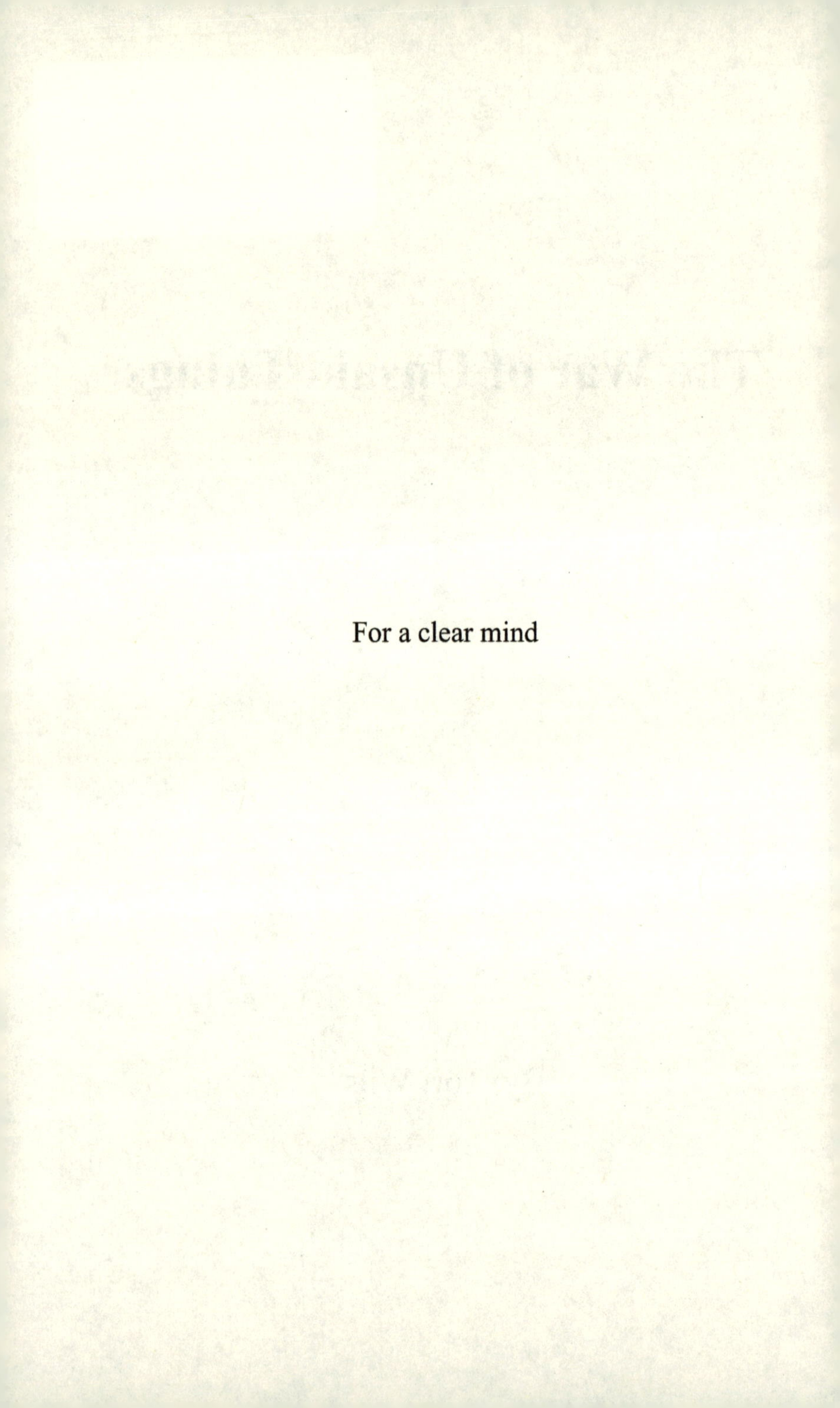

For a clear mind

TABLE OF CONTENTS

SECTION ONE: *WAR IN THE MIND*

SECTION TWO: *WAR IN THE WORLD*

The War of Unsaid Things is a short poetry collection that reveals common themes and emotions in a unique way, allowing for readers to relate to one another across distance and time. This collection works through two sections to give voice to both internal and external thoughts and behaviors.

These pieces of poetry and prose have been split between two sections: War in the Mind and War in the World. Pieces within War in the Mind represent inner emotions and thoughts - how they make us feel, how they are processed, and how they can create or destruct. The words written in this section are those of late-night introspection; the introspection being wanted or not. Pieces within War in the World represent the issues produced by societal expectations or social issues that plague the world we live in. The poems and prose here are based on problems that affect all of us, both individually and as a population.

For example, some of the pieces in War in the Mind center around anxiety, depression, and love. Some pieces in War in the World center around domestic violence, gender inequality, and alcoholism. The topics may range widely, but that is what makes this collection so special - it connects the pieces to us through common, shared human experiences. My hope is that these pieces will expose to every reader just how connected we are, especially in uneasy times.

SECTION ONE:
WAR IN THE MIND

Fearful Phoenix

Feeling fearful is unbecoming,
a sensation tingling through your body,
when you realize existence is temporary.
The after never experienced,
an unknown world awaits our presence,
yet a presence is that amongst the unknown.
I've become, became, uncome, uncame, and
still, I fail, falling perish to broken beacons of
faulted promises and prayers.
Fear burns to rage within a know-it-all
with no answers while
reassurances hold no weight.
Weightless in re temporary, fight for the
spotlight: they tie for equal emptiness.
Rage burns out to fear once more,
leaving the ashes of a fearful phoenix,
with one life left.

Old Wounds

She tore the skin
from her fingertips
until bone peaked through -
raw flesh, open wounds
- *old wounds* -
ripped apart, part of
why she cries at night while
words sit on her tongue -
stuck on the tip
pressing against her lips,
curled inside trembling
through her as muscles tense
at the way her mind won't
stop thinking of
- *old wounds* -
right when her voice
won't start speaking
out loud but to herself.

Always to herself.

Just be - For you

The sun and the moon rise again and again but know when it's time to rest. They wait for you, then rise again. The stars burn bright against the black canvas of nothingness and don't drown in it, but belove it. They don't demand light but create it - for you. Even in your darkest hour, there is a star using its last bit of light, dying proudly - for you. The birds dance within the breeze - for you. Hoping you'll want to be just as free. Free and dreaming of the day you'll see yourself the way you were born into this world, not how the world is intending for you to be seen.

The world demands nothing from you, it only desires - for you.

Unconditional Love

Yes. Hear it and listen. Slowly take
this in - the earth loves you.
It gives everything needed for
instinct and imagination and
asks for one thing in return
- your presence for one more day.

9:59

Red skies full of blood and
tears formed on the banks of puffed
skin - breaking off in pieces, not shattering,
just sinking into the dark clouds on the inside
and his heart burns every time he
thinks to himself;

It's quite lonely here.

Insomniac

Clock strikes ten, you lie in bed clothed and covered
in constant warmth while raindrops drizzle beside your
ear, leaving only comfort and faint breaths.
Within the hour, everything changes, mind fair game
to man-made stories and recollections.
Clock strikes eleven, your legs grow restless
and your body forgets tomorrow.
The song in the rain long gone leaving
only darkness though your eyes wide open,
lullabies jumping for joy, but then -

clock strikes one, your head is pounding.
The summer secrets and the lullabies
washed away for only thoughts of future
failures after midnight are here to stay.

Toxic Mind

Their mind is lost,
they struggle inside.
The pain's like frost,
they're letting go, they tried.

Their heart is heavy,
the ground is shaking -
They'll never be ready,

who was I faking?

Life keeps rushing,
but they are overflowing.
How can they keep trusting,

how do I keep going?

Taste of Repose

True release is felt when the mind is eased
and all nerves relinquished. It's the color of blue.
The rush of a wave of Prussian calming
never-ending thoughts.

It's the indigo hue of the midnight sky,
encompassing every skin cell,
drowning out the world while it sinks you
deeper into the feeling of freeness. Like
the smoked silver of a blue jay's whistle,
nothing else matters once the serene sound
rings through your bones – hushing their own rattle.

It's the brisk breeze against your cheek on a winter day.
The body shuts down around a world of unsaturated blues,
leaving only the lingering effects of quietude.

The Willow Tree

Walk to the willow,
see what you find.
Walk to the willow,
let go of your mind.
Walk to the willow,
there is treasure to be found.
Walk to the willow,
you're close when it sounds.
Walk to the willow,
listen and learn.
Walk to the willow,
for the answers for which you yearn.
Walk to the willow,
and she'll tell you life's not fair.
Walk to the willow,
and she'll tell you love is rare.

Walk to the willow,
for her advice will help repair.
Walk to the willow,
for the truth if you dare.

Un-lasting Love

36 years later, she went home hoping
the initials carved into the sycamore
were there; yet the tree was but a stump.
Like her lover, it was gone, but the deep
rooted memory of it all remained like residue.

Cataclysmic Bond

No other battles rage fiercer than ours
for our explosions ceaselessly desire to
tear and pull and cut and shoot and kill, till
the other retreats – living to fight again.

No battlefield more battered and bruised than
that where we lay, pray, eat, and sleep - For the
four walls holding the cries of victory and defeat
have withered away to dust and fallout.

No flame burning more feral and frenzied,
bloodthirsty for more chaos and ruin,
than the one within our hearts that yearn to
clash and caress in chronic civil war.

Yet, even when bombs drop, your passion,
your voice, your fight is a white flag flying.

Letter for Morrow's Night

If the moon will rise
on the day I die, know
that it is me.

Shining down,
with a swelling smile
waiting for you
to join me in
this peace.

I'll be waiting for
that gracious day
when we can meet
again, and press play.

But do not rush tomorrow
for the delay will
mean more stories
from you that I may borrow.

Though the days may feel heavy,
do not fret. Just know
that I am waiting for you
somewhere happiness overflows.

If the moon will rise
on the day I die, know
that it is me.

Wanting the World, But Not Enough

The sky swallowed me,
the clouds cried out;

"It is almost over."

One more cold,
earthly day felt on
my numb cheeks
-burning red, stained
and bruised.

"Just one more day,
It is almost over."

Breathless air rushing
against my skin,
ocean waves curling
around my body.
A body of water
drowning another.
The mountains roared
through my bones
at that moment,

"It is almost over."

One less scorching,
yearning day burning
tattoos of pigment
from the sun.

The world went silent.

Wanting the World Enough

The sky swallowed me, and the clouds cried out, "you can do this". One more cold, earthly day felt on my numb cheeks -burning red, stained, and bruised. *You can make it, just one more day.* Breathless air rushing against my skin, ocean waves curling around my body. A body of water drowning another. The mountains roared through my bones and at that moment, "you can do this", resonated. One more scorching, earthly day burning tattoos of pigment from the sun.

Losing Our Marrow

The sound of rings and dings and unfamiliar voices are unsettling to hear when awaking to the light. My fingers quiver by my side, gripping white sheets and then a clipboard with the words: JANE DOE. I was her – a blank slate. An empty frame with no memories held within. White coats rushed in, confused at my lack of panic. Questions blurted: "Who are you?" "What happened?". It was my voice that quivered now, fighting the brace
holding it, constricting it, back, "you, they, and them." You were them and them were you, society – devouring my identity to its marrow and leaving the frame lost to the cruel pressures
of the world, draped over as normalcy. JANE DOE, a frame with no identity or depth, just a pariah in a paradigm. "Amnesia" the white coats say. Amnesia –their cover for snuffing the light out, the spark out. JANE DOE: discharged. White sheets and a blue gown traded for a university tee and notebook. The red rain reflecting off the emergency sign stretched wide across blaring lights and black pavement. A world claiming to be boisterous and bold, but submissive to acceptable group conduct. No name, no self, no originality. Only sameness and alignment with mankind. A JANE DOE, one amongst many.

Everchanging Wind

There is survivor's guilt and then there is surviving guilt. The latter is the guilt experienced when being alive has seemed like a chore. The guilt of being alive just because I am, not because I've survived. I'm alive - unworthy of this gift when I have nothing to give.

But that is an idea that creeps its way into the minds of the most creative, the most ambitious, the ones who think outside of the sphere underfoot. That thought squeezes into our unorganized brains and threatens our perseverance because we are too great and too worthy of being stuck in a box; a set of rules - the ones set in place by a collective of stick types, the straight and narrow.

Be the everchanging wind that picks up the sticks with ease and shakes the leaves off of the trees.

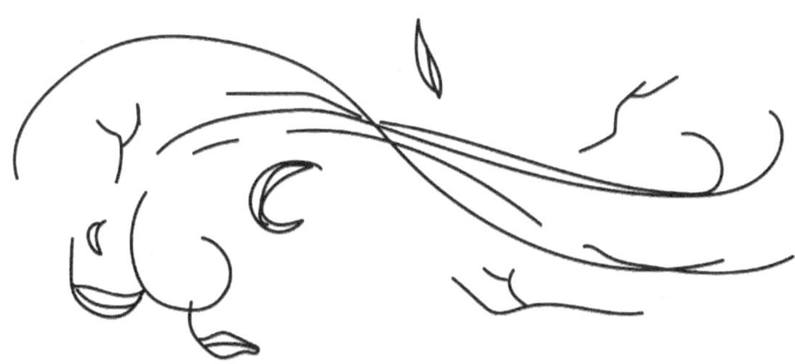

SECTION TWO:
WAR IN THE WORLD

Human Desire for Immortal Narrative

Listen for the bellowing cries as you walk past the faceless desert and
empty words written on gray slabs of stone holding
untold stories buried with lovers, fighters, friends, and
Henrietta Lacks, James Armistead, Amelia Bloomer,
Thomas Clarkson, Irena Sendler who
taken by disease or hatred or love or a hamartia, lived.
I can hear the untold stories crying out from the cemetery and
I can feel them begging to be told and heard and cherished
in fear that the life we lived will cease to dent the sphere we walk on, yet
gone is not the fear, but more so forgotten.
Who will share the stories of a beloved father or devoted wife -
from life till death, accomplishing the only guarantee of us all.
What are we if not a story told by words and numbers -
an infinity of life within a bound set needing to be expressed
through love and fear, courage and dreams,
action and reaction - life is created by more of its own.
Life and story are the same and they must be shared
or they both end without a purpose,
but he who was once alive will remain if his story,
now buried beneath earth and soil, goes on.

Blind Obedience

What I was taught to believe - now reality

I crave your skin on mine,

you know what they say about the juice and the berries.

Without you, I am drowning like a fish out of water - useless,

but still useful,
because like that fish, I can still provide a master a good meal.

Don't be afraid- I just wanna hold you tight,

you came tonight.
Not by pleasure or will, but look at you standing tall.

Boy, don't fear me - the ones that came before you claim to not feel any more pain.

If I let go, will you give up?
Stand now, swing later. My hole lusts for your melanin.

We have something in common, we're both in knots at the core.

You will always be my favorite.

Unforgotten Cries

Unforgiving knowledge
unbearable,
we push the thoughts down to -

what they call insomnia,
I call a cycle of painful regrets.

Hell is what their lives are,
A life lived not asked to live.

Hear their screams, heed their
calls,
unheard voices withering before
us.

Abused, neglected, unloved,
used only once, yet -

We cherish a purebred,
even when we are not so.

Through tears I cannot forget,
I cannot help them all.

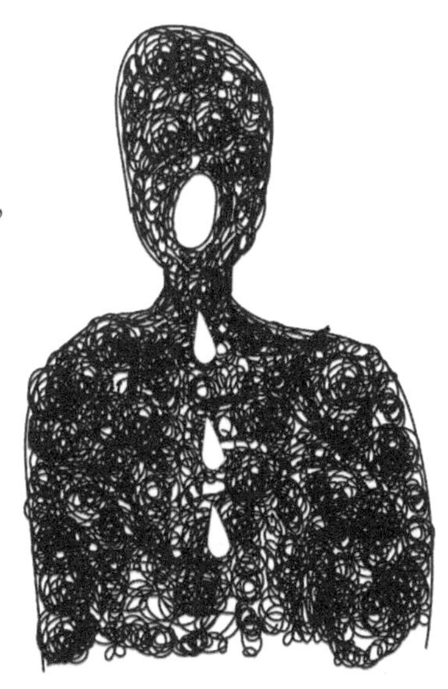

Lies of the Lotus Eaters

They all say what a time to be alive
and say it with pride, but it's all just
a lie like distractions and picture-perfect pictures
on screens and you don't seem to see
what's in my head, it's all just screams,
but they say it's the time to be alive.
It's all just a lie -
all the lies told by lotus eaters,
making us focus on irrelevance
so we won't be leaders -
leaders of revolutions, leaders of movements.
"If you lead, you'll be the one in the tomb"
next - you think it's just a text
but all those texts stop you
from being your best so
focus on your own success.

Church and State *after Gwendolyn Brooks*

You preach on a stage created before your time
spewing words that make no sense so you seem cool,
but you see, your power is dangerous when you talk to young boys
just leaving school. You professor words of wisdom and insight.
Maybe even words that paralyze, just so they'll stay late.
Yet you swear that you and everyone else must remain straight.
The Bible says God will strike down those who commit sin, so I wonder,

when is He coming for you?

You drink your gin
in your office, offering them some in exchange for silence.
The church found out what you've been doing late at night.
You've planned to move to a new church in June. They'll cover it up
and now you'll have new boys to choose from soon.

Carving a Valley of Sin

We enter the world innocent.
No wrongs have been made -
only tears shed,
smiles spread.

As we grow, we learn.
Experiencing the world -
the light and the dark,
seeking our spark.

We learn on our own.
Like a child left alone -
acting with disobedience,
mindless expedience.

Not only are we carving a valley of sin,
but we enhance our knowledge of wrong.
We may choose a rough path but,
we were not made to pursue perfection.

They call us the youth.

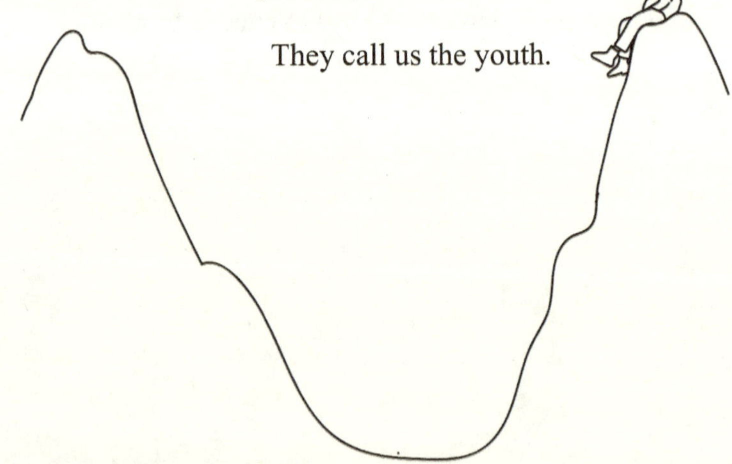

Done Me Wrong

You gotta
pick a path.
Pick a prick to
pry with,
To pick apart a
person's
apartment.
You gotta
pick a path.
A pal to
puff with,
pick a lock with.
I picked a path -
a person to pilfer,
to pop,
to pummel,
and ended up
picked up.

One Parent Down

His first words as a man charged guilty
were mouthed to the 1-year-old gripping
her mother, "I'll regret the next decade that
I must spend away from you. You are loved."
His first steps followed and with it the clinking
of regretful chains.

Violence from the Less Domestic

You're like rain on my windowpane. Sounds flooding my ears, devouring my thoughts with melancholy memories of - you are like the ground that I walk on, stable and level. You are my protector, promising to keep me safe, away from terrifying fates of the world. You are all these things - yet you strike with unwarranted wrath and speed. The ground is shaking and I'm losing my balance. The heat from the center of the earth is rising through the cracks in the ground getting ready to explode while the soles on my shoes are burning out layer by layer. As my feet

begin to melt and as my lungs begin to fill with the breath that will not leave my chest, I can see

the light behind me, but my feet are already gone, and I cannot run, I cannot move, I cannot

breathe.

You have taken over every inch of my body from the inside out. You've cut out every ounce of my connection with breathing beings. I can use my arms to try and crawl towards the light before I get sucked into the crack forever, I can. *Try.* But my arms will burn against that harsh concrete, and I will have nothing left

And while I have nothing, you will have it all. You will have my feet, my arms, my heart and soul, my light because *you* are my earth, and I am just something you will devour through your hell of a core.

Black Button Eyes

Blood rushing,
heart pumping,
head spinning,
palms sweating,

The signs of –
panic sets in when
she sees the color
of *you*.

Glaring red skin,
burrowed-out eyes,
black buttons
like Coraline's.

Empty.
Alone.
Not home.

This is it,
where it ends.
"THIS IS ALL ON YOU",
too late for amends.

Familial Heartbreak

One first face I saw in this world.

Fresh face like fresh wounds even on
days that feel forgotten and far, far away.
You broke more than just bones and
burst more than just blood vessels,
branded more than just burns,
buried more than just secrets,
busted more than just black eyes,
bruised more than just flesh.

You were one of the first faces
I saw in this world,
one of the first people I loved,
one of the first set of arms to hold me,
one of the first to make me laugh,
yet you caused so much pain.

Pain that doesn't feel forgotten or far, far away.
Pain that's not supposed to be mine, but I feel it anyway.

You were my family. You *broke* my family.
They may have forgiven you,
but I have the luxury to not have to.

Guilty of Disease

"Arson is a crime against property. It is the burning and destruction of something. Assault is a crime against persons. It is the infliction of pain and hurt on someone. Weapon law violations are a crime against society. It is the abuse and use of a lethal object without permission. Drunkenness is a crime against society. It is…it's a…it's the state of being drunk. Too drunk. Too drunk to function in society, yes. Too drunk to walk in a straight line, yes. Too drunk to comprehend, yes. Too drunk that this is what we condemn, yes. This is behavior not worthy of our country. We declare now that if one is too drunk, it is a crime against society."

But what of those who cannot help it? What of those who are ill, or alcohol bends their will, or they make a deal not to drink until they can't keep that promise any longer? We sentence them to a charge they do not deserve, but yes, you've done so in the name of society. For our own good, the survival of the community. Survival of the fittest. We thrive without the drunken roaming the streets, wasted, and wasting their time away, withering before our eyes. But yes, we watch and wait for their suffering to end at their own hand, in the name of society. In the name of society, we have declared alcoholism a crime. In the name of society, we have decreed a disease of the brain a crime.

"What is done is done. Let us not dwell on the complexities. They must learn that drunkenness is wrong, that addiction is wrong, that disease is wrong, that they can be fixed through time served. Stuff them all in one big box so the "disease" is free of us, one we cannot contract. Maybe the "disease" will die off or better yet, maybe the "disease" will only be caught by the ones deserving of it. This is their own fault; why should society suffer for their lack of self-control, or their poor judgment calls? For their choice to abuse what the rest of us enjoy in moderation?"

We put disease in quotations as if alcoholism is not so. Some abuse, while others use, because it's medicinal to their pain. Their trauma becomes buried when they are drowning under the influence. Their hurt becomes numb, and they don't feel the toll that their life has on them. We drink in moderation because we don't feel that pain, that trauma, that hurt. We drink to feel alive; they drink as part of a fight for a will to live. We judge them for this disease, but we – the society with no fault or fractures – are part of the reason for their addiction. We criminalize their behavior, but we – the society that needs protection from the struggling human beings within it – are part of the reason they do not have access to the help they need. We – the society that is perfect and clean and can do no wrong – have let down the friends and family and strangers who need us the most.

"Drunkenness and alcoholism do not belong here. Society is the victim to their crimes."

No. Society is a crime against humanity. It is the destruction of the people within it.

10:09

Am I sharing this existence
but for a single purpose?
Numbers -
worth measured in numerals and gossip.
Sharing beautiful space with
pain-bearing burdened bags of bones and judgment.
She's a bag of bones and judgment.
Words -
breaking the strongest of steel.

Am I sharing this existence with a bag of bones and judgment
just to break like steel from numbers and words as she measures my worth
in numerals and gossip?

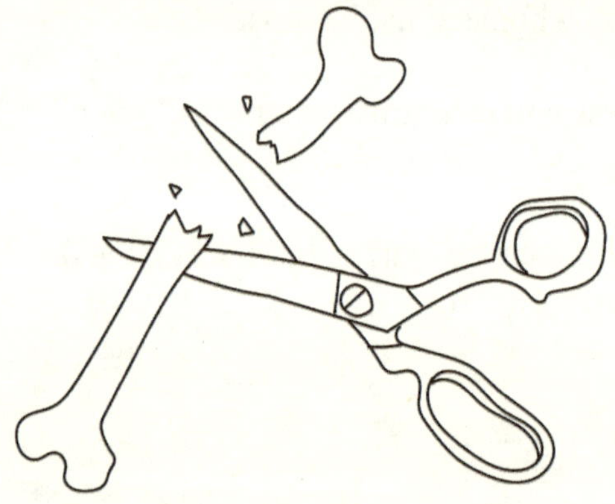

A Man's World

Scorching air surrounds his body.
A burning breeze rushing against me
while he sits around like he's so godly.
Craving more like the average man,
desiring a life with the demand of now.
His heart heavy with greed ever since he began
to lie and cheat and steal, and sin.
Like he always says, "I receive what I desire
with my hands and my grin."

Daughters of Athena

Athena. Goddess of Wisdom, yes, but also a goddess of war. We forget that fact. We like to separate Athena and Ares: the woman is the brain, and the man is the muscle, but that is a false generalization. Yes, Athena, Goddess of Wisdom, was also the provider of courage. She could bring courage and relieve it all in the same day. Hercules and Perseus, famous for their feats, but Athena was their creditor. She was the creator of purpose and imagination, an extinguisher of Ares' flames. She'd protect the weak, bring advancement, and slay the enemy all in one. The spear and shield are her passion, and she wore THAT on her sleeved cloak. Her body - her own - and she would end anyone who'd cowardly try to change that fact. She was fierce, every day. She was worthy, every day. She embodied power, every day. She was a force and a reckoning, every day. Both brain and brawn, intelligence and strength, beauty and build; she was fearful of no man in a man's world. She was the Goddess Athena, every day. Unlike what we've been conditioned to believe, we are not the daughters of Aphrodite - the simplified version of her story that we have been told, just beauty and seduction - we are the daughters of Athena.

Barbie Doll

Burn away white cotton cloth
and polished china.
Hair slicked back
no longer, but longer it is – blonder.

Always pose. Smile for the camera.
Hands tucked away from wandering eyes,
shy and shy and shy and shy.
Shy, no longer – but hands out wide.

Ruffles and ribbons,
Still white cotton cloth.
Cut it in two,
expose with shimmering silver.

Old dreams burning away,
Not in disgust nor angst, not even grief,
But a need longer.
For it is complete.

Time passes as if it even existed,
From 4 to 24 – black and white no longer.
Embrace the pink with passion,
Roses and ribbons and fire and power.

From little to old,
a little too old,
changes forever changing.
Our temples may grow,
and novelty persists, but vision never strains.

Fierce and a beauty,

Power and delicacy, young and strong.
Surviving in a world built
against her.

Knew her vision as a young girl,
grew into her vision now.
They say we are what we eat.
And she ate a barbie cake

I am a Forest Fire

Come -
She thought,
see me and let's be

Embers in trees,
prancing with the wind
as her dress burns
through society's looking glass.

Magnified on her errors,

she dances on their reflection –
I am the fire you seek,
more than beauty. I am power.

But the world wants half of her;
discard vigor and skill, capability –
they want modest seductress.

Come –
She thought,
see me. Seek
more than beauty.
Like fire to trees,
I make embers prance
through wind -
I am power.

I am a forest fire in society.

ABOUT THE AUTHOR

Tori Wils is the pen name of writer and poet, Jayla Wilson. This is her first self-published work, with a second poetry collection in progress. She has a blog called *A Mixed Perspective*. Follow her online to stay updated on upcoming projects.

TikTok: amixedperspective
Instagram: _amixedperspective
Blog: https://amixedperspective.wixsite.com/web1

www.ingramcontent.com/pod-product-compliance
Lightning Source LLC
LaVergne TN
LVHW090538110826
845146LV00003B/1170

* 9 7 9 8 2 1 8 2 3 0 9 1 3 *